THE
POWER OF A
WOMAN'S
WARDROBE

Cassandra Harmon

authorHOUSE

AuthorHouse™
1663 Liberty Drive
Bloomington, IN 47403
www.authorhouse.com
Phone: 1 (800) 839-8640

Published by AuthorHouse 11/30/2019

ISBN: 978-1-7283-3742-5 (sc)
ISBN: 978-1-7283-3740-1 (hc)
ISBN: 978-1-7283-3741-8 (e)

Library of Congress Control Number: 2019919574

Print information available on the last page.

Any people depicted in stock imagery provided by Getty Images are models, and such images are being used for illustrative purposes only. Certain stock imagery © Getty Images.

Scripture taken from The Holy Bible, King James Version. Public Domain

Scripture quotations marked NIV are taken from the Holy Bible, New International Version®. NIV®. Copyright © 1973, 1978, 1984 by International Bible Society. Used by permission of Zondervan. All rights reserved. [Biblica]

This book is printed on acid-free paper.

Because of the dynamic nature of the Internet, any web addresses or links contained in this book may have changed since publication and may no longer be valid. The views expressed in this work are solely those of the author and do not necessarily reflect the views of the publisher, and the publisher hereby disclaims any responsibility for them.

Contents

Acknowledgments

Great gratitude is expressed for the friends who encouraged the production of this work. As a natural introvert, and one who appreciates privacy, many years of suggestion and contemplation were required to arrive at this place. Thank you R. Theodore Wilson III and Raaedah Abdussabuur for being resolute supports in my life. Many do not understand the nature of the friendships; yet, I appreciate the intangible gifts that you have given to me. Thank you, again.

Warm regards are also offered to the amazing teachers and professors who influenced me at Saint Mark's High School and Wilmington University. Building a strong vocabulary and a civic awareness were cornerstones of my primary education. Receiving professional recognition and maturation of those tenets during my secondary phase forged a competence and a confidence to communicate boldly and effectively. Special thanks are shared with Ms. Rachel Ali and Dr. David Farmer, respectively. Those brief moments have rippled throughout my lifetime.

Lastly, I give the highest praise to God. Spiritual studies have given me a clear perspective: life offers trials and triumphs to all of us. My belief in God has been my sanctuary through horrible storms. It has kept my mind stayed. Moreover, my optimism comes from my experience. Great things have happened for me despite transgressions. Every part of life has value. Learning to appreciate the peaks and troughs gives amazing perspective and peace. It allows me to stand resolutely today.

Introduction

It was told that ladies shouldn't discuss certain things. Well, being a lady became tiresome and trite. A host of secret things are found between these pages.

The female voice is strong, and the words are clear. May women and men, alike, resonate with the echoes and begin to sway. A raw rhythm beats on this drum. Power is best girded by truth.

The Power Suit

The power suit is a statement piece. It represents who you are with visual appeal and a sublime proclamation. Some like a traditional black or blue suit, perhaps tailored well or with a pin stripe pattern for a bit of sophistication. Others like an ostentatious appeal, flamboyant and stunning – simply to captivate onlookers by a wild nature or strategically planned to be memorable. How do you display your success to the world?

The power suit is a power move. It identifies your place and your position. Leaders can be found everywhere – on the frontlines, in back room operations, and within high-level administrative suites. While the place of influence is unique, and the available resources may differ, power is ultimately used for the same purpose – to create change. That change may benefit one or it may benefit many. Influence may be wielded in community governance meetings, at business engagements, in the home, and on street corners. Where is your success meaningful?

The power suit is your assimilated focus. It is the fulfilled integration of ideas, people, and cultures. Authority is designated through purpose, whether granted or taken. Your power enables intention to become action. When do you walk and talk with power?

If you don't have a power suit, get one! Every day offer opportunities to build your place of power.

The word of a powerful man is the truth. ~Bambara Proverb

Painted Lady

~Observations of media and women

I wear a sculpted, painted, burnished mask, feather-fringed with peacock colors:

Red - passionate and furious
Green - prosperous and life-affirming
Gold - royal and mined deep within
Blue - saddened and serene
Black - culminating all colors to the pride of my womanly strength

I cover myself in garb, loose with natural textures, preparing the days to come with a multitude of pre-empted gestures.

Cotton, wool, and silken blends of name-brand clothes and other trends: exploiting my body and constricting my mind - to believe that sluttiness, lewdness, and whoredom are fine.

Leather, fur, Gucci and Prada: all stretching my wallet - and limiting my ideas - of what I gotta... BE... to be beautiful.

Have you those models: slim, airbrushed, rare, and cool-eyed? Whoever said, "good things come in small packages" spoke a partial truth or told a goddamn lie.

That narrow runway could never bear the weight of my big nose, big butt, big hips, and big thighs. Yet, I continue to spend, for the sake of my image demised.

I'm ready for war, or should I say I'm dressed to kill? I'm gonna find me a man and make him bend at will. For the sake of this battle, I gots to be right; cuz you better believe I'm gonna gets me a man or borrow one tonight!

Out at the club, the hunt begins: stealthy moves along the strip, at the store, or anywhere else there might be some mens.

My body is toned. My mind is set. My spirit is removed, cuz my pussy is wet.

Honey, I am fierce! I know I won't be alone tonight... cuz my self-image is shallow and my hair weave is tight! That man won't know what he's gettin' cuz I couldn't tell him myself... and God knows I sound stupid sometimes when I open my mouwf.

But that's okay, there's a reason why I wear my mask. It bears all my true colors, and it hides my past. All the shame, insecurities, hurts and fears stay here, behind my mask, where no one sees the tears.

So, I wear my mask to remind me of me. And when I see those breath-taking colors in the mirror, I remember...

I wear a sculpted, painted, burnished mask, feather-fringed with peacock colors:

Red - passionate and furious
Green - prosperous and life-affirming
Gold - royal and mined deep within
Blue - saddened and serene
Black - culminating all colors of the pride of my womanly strength

---

Because I've Been Broken

Because I've been broken, I am...
Wild and free
Cloaked and distant
Intelligent and pensive
Beautiful and poised
Direct and brazen

Charming and seductive
Full and abounding
Compassionate and supportive
Teacher and student
Lover and friend
Child and mother
All things embraced

Because I've been broken, I am...
Who I am
Not who you want me to be
Void of shame
Immune to social validation
Aware of self
A summation of experiences - heard, seen, smelled, tasted, and
touched
All things me

Because I've been broken, I am...
Blood, tears, anguish
Birth, death, reincarnation
Binding, breaking, restoring
Happiness, joy, contentment
Selfish, selfless, unmoved
Ignorant, knowledgeable, wise
Dissention, chaos, order
Natural, branded, packaged
All things authentic

Because I've been broken, I am...
Creating my own world and loin cloth, blissfully colored and textured to suit my tastes
Standing alone in a crowd, enthralled by interactions and pleased with the clear view
Choosing the information sources, mediums that speak truth and nourish my soul
Vibrating at a different frequency, elevated and broad
All things powerful

Because I've been broken
I am who I am

W.I.T.C.H.

Women
In
Truth
Channeling
Healing

We, as women, must define who we are. Equally important is creating the context in which we are perceived. The concept of a witch has been so negatively stigmatized over centuries that women succumb to partial truths and fail to honor their true nature.

A witch was a woman known to be wise. She understood how to use plants and herbs to heal; she aided the birthing of children; she cultivated her own land; she was knowledgeable about crafting at home; she was skilled in trade in the marketplace; and she was deeply spiritual. These things happened with – or without – the presence of a man. A wise woman had the capacity to be self-sufficient if she chose to do so.

Female energy and power if often minimalized and dishonored. It is exhibited in the simplest of phrases, like "running like a girl," to the grandest of gestures, like being burned on stakes and beaten in streets. A basic truth is suffocated. Yet, very few ask why that truth is suffocated.

Women have power. If we are all created in the likeness of a divine being (whatever you choose to call that higher sense of self) is power not an attribute of God or Gaia? As one rules the Heaven, another rules the Earth. In science (i.e. the systematic study of the natural and physical order of the world), balance – or the process thereof – is something that is constantly working to be achieved. There is generally a positive and a negative aspect. With respect to polarity, the positive/giving side is ascribed to the male part, where the negative/receiving side is ascribed to the female counterpart. Both are needed to maintain balance. If too much of a thing exists on one side, it can cause imbalance. The excess should be released and shared with a viable counterpart to maintain the goal of balance.

Given the afore-mentioned thoughts, should it not seem reasonable to move beyond the pure studies of science to the applied versions of science? If the aspect of the male/man is a giver status [of resources], it seems reasonable to deduce that the aspect of the female/woman is the receiver status [of given resources]. A further assumption is that the female aspect receiving resources will assimilate or manage the components to be productive and bring balance. This concept should synchronously flow from the science lab, to the church sanctuary, to the interiors of homes, as well as other environments. Ironically, it does not.

A woman can have resources and influence when she operates in her naturally created state. Women acquire. Women plan. Women delegate. Women employ. Women create. Women, recognize and receive the blessings brought before you. Appreciate and employ your power wherever you are positioned.

Push Back

You left me to fight for myself
Now, you're angry that I wear red boxing gloves
And push back

When The Freak Stepped Out

When the freak stepped out
The woman stepped in
Although they appear very close
Be known, they are very different kin

The freak might lay with you for free
The woman will make you pay at the door
Should she give you anything at less than cost
Trust and believe, there's nothing more

Don't look for insights or suggestions of anything deeper
The woman understood
It was only something cheaper
That his pocket could afford

As such, nothing surmounts but moments passed
The woman accepts a whimsical time
Like the dreams of knights and fairies
Nothing substantial to last

When the freak stepped out
The woman stepped in
Full of confidence, full of comfort, full of passion
And sprinkled with a little sin

Female Savage

Writing sets me free from the cages of my mind. Secrets locked behind doors - pushed down and silenced - many of no desire to find.

Did you hear the screams in the corner (or perhaps down the hall)? My daddy died at the whim of a research center, an institution renowned and admired by all.

A young man vowed to protect me, but instead, ravished my youth. Two boys said to themselves, "let's get it," and I became the object of a lecherous uncouth.

Adolescence was difficult. Even as a young adult, relationships were bad, at best. Believers continually speaking platitudes that God is preparing me for great things; hence, the reasons for these tests.

I used to pray for strength - until I realized that it brought nothing more than burdens. The process of becoming something new - in this case a creature borne - a metamorphosis - the Germanic act of werden.

Now, I ask for wisdom and peace; knowledge applied; and a sound mind stayed. In this state, understanding that strategy and skill are the tools needed to slay the beasts and craft gratifying days.

Monsters have lived in my mind. Their damage took root in my heart. Breaking yokes, aged at more than 20 years, has proven well-deserving of a brand, new start.

It became clear that reflection and repositioning were needed for true relief. Incisors must be sharpened to tear, cut, or crush the bone and marrow of the thief.

Acknowledge what was felt; what was lost; the guidance never had. Understand that some things are out of one's control. What is chosen, nonetheless, is what one perceives as either good or that of bad.

You, you persons, both male and female alike, took parts of me to make yourselves comfortable. In response, the lash of my tongue, the acrid taste and smell of my truth, shall be spit before you and make your place insufferable.

Heavy residues of maliciousness dripped into my eyes. It covered the base of my soul, and I struggled to see any light. Lost in a torrent of shadows, I feared myself, not fully aware of a matured girth and might.

Now, void of guilt and void of shame, I stand before you, strong and erect. Be fully warned, this is the only notice, civility and refinement got put in check.

The memory of me returned. The cage is open, and the female savage is loose.

PERSONAL POWER QUESTIONS: POWER SUIT

1. What is the image of your ideal power suit?
2. Do you currently own a power suit? If yes, when do you choose to wear it?
3. When do you feel powerful?
4. Where is your circle of influence (where can you make change)?
5. Are powerful people and leaders the same or different? Explain why or why not?

Cleaning Clothes

Dirty jobs are rarely chosen, yet they serve a purpose. The same goes for the clothes needed to attend the work. Individuals and corporations involved in dirty environments recognize and anticipate a level of undesirable grime related to the job. Preparations are made accordingly. Everything must be cleaned from time-to-time, from homes, to hospitals, to industrial sites. Specialized care may be taken, like personal protective equipment (PPE) or hazardous material (hazmat) removal procedures. Other times, basic cleaning clothes can be worn to attend the routine muck of the days.

Cleaning clothes are designated to accommodate any dirt, dust, or harsh agents that might damage skin or other less protective clothing. There's also an unstated rule that cleaning clothes are not to be worn in public places. You may ask why such a rule exists. It stands because the clothes are unsightly. Common hallmarks of these items are ill-fitting fabric, holes, and stains.

This part of a woman's wardrobe is rarely discussed, because the items are unsightly (like the old panties with bad elastic). No one wants to admit or claim ownership of the ugly things that exist in their closets, bureaus, and storage units. Unfortunately, the same holds true for the ugly things that happen in our lives. In this moment, appreciate the old sweatpants, ragged jeans, faded head scarves, and paint-stained shirts that allow you to work through the mess. Hopefully, it's a short-lived task; and, your space is changed for the better once the work is done!

Beautiful Sun

Today was a day when I thought about the way we used to be, sweet in the beautiful sun and brown from its rays.

Our plump and supple fruit was becoming withered, like Muscat grapes of entangled vines that dry to the raisins form.

We were in the light and the warmth of the beautiful sun. Pleasantries of life became hard to discern - perhaps the sunlight distorted our view. Things that seemed natural and free gradually became artificial and taxed.

Our eager souls stammered at the attempts to endure.

Sunny days became hot. The heat caused sweat to drip from our brows. The moisture stung when it caressed out eyes.

Our temperaments were no longer mild.

We still held hands in the face of the beautiful sun. Like all things that are cold, our bond remained tight.

While we embraced and coveted many dark things, the beautiful sun's beams reached across the sky with a fierce energy and danced feverishly about us.

Our bond was broken by the kinetic movement.

The beautiful sun melted the icy junctures that kept us together - fear, manipulation, aggression, and abuse. These things were born of the fruit of ignorance. We were no longer beautiful.

Our separateness was exposed by the beautiful sun's gleaming rays.

Today was a day when I thought about the way we used to be, and I am ever thankful the beautiful sun continues to shine.

God has brought me through many things. This is my prayer. Amen.

Black And Red Pinstripe Pants And Silver Bangle Bracelets

Two-on-one, presumably friends
You stole my innocence, and called yourselves men
Youth offending youth
Semen mingled with muffled groans and tears in a school basement
Boys learning about themselves
A girl learning about life, impersonal and faceless

You switch, like the baton traded during a meet of track and field
Running for the goal, to get that rush
Never once thinking to yield
A bursting sensation released, the byproduct of lust
My mind racing in synch with your rhythms
Simply to escape the unjust

It is over
You take yourselves away from me
My value lost between dangling belts, muffled cries, and open zippers
Thighs wet from a pleasure that was not mine
Alas, teen age boys, serial killers of virtue
The monarch of Jack the Ripper

Homeward bound, alone
Through the city's dark, concrete field an array of scents fill the nostrils

Voices and memories echo around me
A blooming 13-year-old girl accosted

I can hear the blood pulsing through my veins
And never stop to feel or listen
I wore black and red pinstripe pants
And silver bangle bracelets

Things You're Told

Things family members told me as a little girl...
You're fat
You didn't do it right
You'll never make anything of yourself
I can't help you
Deafening silence in response to a verbal expression of love

Things I told myself as an adult...
You're beautiful
You do extraordinary work
You've accomplished many things
Help is available when you need it (ask God to show you where)
You are loved

Being open and receptive to the abundance of good things in life was hard to receive because it was hard to see. My heart and vision are clearer now. The things you are told can crush or catapult your spirit. You choose.

Eve's Rape

Eve, can you remember...
When sight was irrelevant?
When the universe was small?
When ignorance was acceptable?

Eve, can you remember...
When the edges of the Garden weren't visible?
When the land was fertile?
When the seeds were planted?

Eve, can you remember...
When your natural beauty was embraced?
When the leaves of the treetops covered the floors of Heaven?
When the underbrush served as a respite place for you?

Do you remember when fruit was pleasant, pungent, and sweet?

Eve replied, I remember my trust...
Before I could see the gate at the edges of the Garden.

Before my womb was plowed by the worldliness of men.
Before his sin covered my glory with a loincloth.

I remember fruit being plucked, and the barren branches that remained.

------◆◆◆------

Barren

Hope has been left void
Desire has gone unfulfilled
Love has rejected the affection
Joy has been stripped
Promise has been suffocated
Labor has born a still birth
Nothing is in this place

------◆◆◆------

~ Sometimes, life is so very hard. We grapple with challenges that seem like unscalable mountains. We feel ill-equipped and overwhelmed. The problems seem to chase us and wrestle us to the ground. Finding a way to get over them, under them, or around them is almost unfathomable, especially when more than one crisis exists at a time.

The following memoir is a copy of a text that was sent to a group of trusted friends toward the close of 2017. It is a lamentation about health challenges, and the subsequent problems, that began in 2015 and persisted through that time. The communication is grief expressed about internal struggles with religion and faith. The commentary notes the socially oppressive judgements and systems that work against women, brown-skinned people, and disabled persons. It took hours to draft the text due to significant delays with information processing. The effort didn't matter. The thoughts and feelings needed to be shared — to be purged.

This memoir is a glance at the most difficult moment in my life: a time of feeling helpless and insignificant on December 18, 2017.

A Broken Heart

Friends, I share this (as a group text) because I am at the end of my ability to understand or appreciate... I am struggling with everything - including my faith. I continue to pray, study & try to find hope/guidance/purpose in this culmination of 30+ years of trials (ugly physical, verbal, emotional, sexual & financial violations; epic struggles to support a family as a single parent - including a child who needs tremendous amounts of special attention [that I can no longer muster at this moment] & prejudices that run the gamut from being a woman, brown-skinned, living in the city or the suburbs, and now disabled).

Strength & faith in God has allowed me to push through; to see a lesson and an opportunity in every circumstance, including the incredible fight - clawing, scraping & grappling - for self-worth, identification, added skills and education to be validated - to be "marketable" - to be equal in the workplace and any space... Only to be told that I am now over-qualified for employment... that my willing attempts at self-employment & budding entrepreneurship has been snuffed out with an auto accident that has debilitated me with an array [of] limitations... and that I am too much of one thing, not enough of the other no matter what I do. Added insult & injury are the hosts of health professionals, legal staff, and acquaintances who simply glance at me and tell me that I look fine. Unfortunately, internal injuries & their side affects are not seen (like my concussion, PTSD, nerve damage, pain, convulsions, displaced discs, etc.).

It seems that everything I have hoped for, strived toward, fought against, overcome, muddled through, prayed about, and stood upon has been futile. EVERYTHING has been stripped from me - my health, my home, my finances, and my ability to provide for myself. The desire to fight is almost gone.

In spite of my inability to work (to reasonably sustain myself), my dire need hearing for disability was declined a 2nd time. Notice came this month. I am at the bottom of the well - dismayed & lost. I've tried to encourage other[s] as I try to encourage myself. As a problem-solver, I seem unable to find a way. I am flailing and my heart is profoundly grieved. I send this because I need to vent my disenchantment & disappointment. My heart hurts because I am no longer strong. I am losing hope.

Please help me with anything you can: strong prayers, a real hug, referral to a service center, help finding a home of my own, financial assistance, a ride, encouragement, whatever you can give.

I am empty. I am displaced. I am in need. And honesty, I really want to be left alone for a while…"

***

Lamentation

After all these years, and all these trials
I'm losing my faith in God
And perhaps that's why

***

It is my experience and my opinion that ignorance breeds most social ill-wills. Stereotypes Stereotypes are derived from prejudices. People pre-judge without having a full knowledge of circumstances or context. Lack of true care comes from lack of relevance or cultural competency. Compassion is stifled because no point of reference exists. Until an experience is personalized, there is no regard for the other who befalls calamity. May the wretchedness of the hard-hearted be reckoned. There is no glory or grace in turning a blind eye to what appears irrelevant to you.

What you see is not necessarily what you get. Life does not exist or express itself in boxes and cookie-cut categories. Life is dynamic; it moves. Life is reciprocal; it balances. Life is connected; it joins. Every action – or lack thereof – has a reaction. Its impact is like the continuing ripples of water once a stone has broken the surface.

All things (ex. money, power, contentment, social standing, etc.) ebb and flow. When we learn how to change with it, we can find favorable opportunities in a multitude of directions. As such, let us work for the advancement of ourselves and that of others.

Idioms

Most folks say, 'when it rains it pours.'
Well, my land is barren and I'm thankful for heaven's tears.
Torrents have relentlessly pounded upon me.
I stand fixed among rubble.
Certainly, I must be clean.

A Biblical proverb says, 'don't cast your pearls before swine.'
Well, my wandering feet have sunk in the pig's mud.
Rain has fallen and soaked all that I have.
My diamonds and shekels are sown deep in the ground.
Thankfully, my shit was piled high and served well for compost.

An old cliché says, 'a bird in the hand is better than two in the bush.'
Well, my traveling bags were lost at sea and my albatross fell from my neck.
Summer showers have refreshed me after the deluge of saltwater.

A mansion was built with discarded stones.

Surely, my silos are filled to excess. My family and yours shall be fed.

Personal Power Questions: Cleaning Clothes

1. What makes you comfortable or uncomfortable in sharing awkward or challenging situations about your life?
2. When have you felt like your sense of power was lost, and who or what helped restore that power?
3. Identify a benefit of experiencing hardship?
4. How can a personal trauma in your life be used to work for the betterment of someone else?
5. Do you think trauma/crisis matters should be addressed publicly or in private (ex. social media, lawsuits, etc.)?

Lingerie

In a woman's wardrobe, lingerie is considered a foundation item. The foundation is the most important part of any structure. That ideal holds true for architectural design, office systems, personal relationships, and, yes, even clothing. A woman's wardrobe is built from the inside – out. Her beauty and her character are designed the same way. The selection of lingerie is revealing.

Intimate apparel reflects a woman's personal style. Colors, textures, and patterns offer insights about who she is. Endearments may be displayed with snuggly animals or sentiments of slumber. Her sense of adventure might be trimmed with dainty lace or the kink of crotchless panties. Even still, a woman's feel for comfort can be found in the choice of breathable cotton or smooth synthetics. As style is important, the purpose of lingerie is most considerable too.

Some pieces are bargain finds, and others are high-dollar fancies. Regardless of the cost, women's undergarments serve one to three purposes: to look good, to feel good, or to taste good. (And yes, some skivvies taste good. Edible panties do exist!) A functional piece can be very pretty. This is the intersection where style and purpose meet. While a woman may look and feel ultra-feminine or sexy, most foundation pieces are acquired for comfort, support, or contouring.

A delicate touch is needed when handling a woman's lingerie. All fine and fragile things, whether cotton, silk, leather, or lace, should be handled with care. Lingerie lies closest to a woman's skin and some of the most sensitive areas of her body. These pieces are also the most revealing when no other garment is worn.

Submission

We reunite because you are mine, and I am yours. Our souls were yoked in a time before our being. You were me, and we were one. Fire.

You are the word of my mind, and the spirit of my flesh. You dwell deep in my soul, and I experience your world. Anchor.

We intertwine the essence of who we are. You are God's love, created for me. I am God's delight, created for you. Bow before my king and honor. Bow before your queen and praise. Submit.

Breed

You breed a deep-seated lust in me... And I chose the word 'breed' because it feels like the world should be propagated with something that we create

You breed a deep-seated lust in me... It's a carnal frenzy, amped on ecstasy: a cosmic energy amplified with a mate

You breed a deep-seated lust in me... And I chose the word 'deep-seated' because it is like the strong roots of an old, wise tree

You breed a deep-seated lust in me... It's a spiritual thing, woven throughout galaxies: twin flames burning wild and free

You breed a deep-seated lust in me... And I chose the word 'lust' because there is an emphatic need to relinquish the passion

You breed a deep-seated lust in me... It's a knowledge of self, and of other: designed intricately to elevate with magnificence and fashion

You breed a deep-seated lust in me... And I chose the word 'me' because I am a reflective part of you

You breed a deep-seated lust in me... It's a spoken word, manifested as desired: clairvoyance of senses with a harnessed power to imbue

We are sun and we are moon: both, aspects of the Most High
We are givers and we are receivers: both, bearers of the Light
We are rich in knowledge and carriers of seeds: both, in subtlety
and in might

You breed a deep-seated lust in me… And I love it

Then We Sleep

When the softness of the night covers the remnants of the day,
slowly creep between my sheets – where I lay outstretched for you.
No effort shall be made to move any part of myself, ensuring that
you see every curve and every measure.

Lean in close, so that I miss no part. Hold your power, suspended
deeply between a passionate kiss and a firm embrace where
fingertips clasp at the small of my back.

Caress the softness of my hips and harness the firmness of yourself
at our center. Angle between the thickness of my isle and provoke
a fantasy of rippled waters.

Prepare to be immersed: not a full plunge, like a pike dive into the
ocean, but wade gently, like a leisurely descent into a basin. Give
an inch, so that you can dangle me on a string of pornographic
hope.

Let me feel the fullness of all that you are - not to satisfy - just to heighten the intensity. Retreat quickly, before the siren casts her spell and we lose the art of foreplay and simply fuck.

Use the dexterity of your hands to navigate the swell of my lips until the tributary flows into a river. The moon heeds the mating ritual and witnesses the tides moving for you.

Kiss the delta and taste a juice blended especially for you. This is erotica, on the verge of kinky, but not quite ready to explore a fully unbridled run.

You offer a warm drink to fill my cup. Allow me to savor the fragrance that is most powerful at your core; and, let me whisper in a place so holy that only your spirit and I know what is spoken.

Deep caverns await. While you may imagine the things that an uninhibited individual might conceive, this moment is beyond an unadulterated carnal thrill.

Submerge to the enchantment of senses. Journey into the place of entrainment.

Will you yield in order to receive something that is comparable to none? I shall mount you, like a lioness on her perch: a conquest that gives access to vision and renewal.

Couple yourself with me so that you feel the weight of my rhythm. Pull me closer and share vitality's pulse.

Desire brings forth heat. Give me more work until I feel your exhaustion and risk losing invigoration to the sweetness of sleep.

I am the wind, riding free until I lose myself in the moment. You are the fire, consuming us both in a magnificent light.

Our breath signifies the struggle between pleasure and persistence. We grind until the metal sticks. Then we sleep.

Missing You

Missing you, like the last flight, and now I'm on standby

Caramel-Coated Candy Apple

I crave you like the sweetness of a caramel-coated candy apple. Your tone is like warm, moist heat on the cusp of erotica, creating a fire in me and a feverishness that quickens the pace of my breath.

Images and words invigorate my mind, while distant miles leave me yearning for margarita kisses – the essence of you brimming over my cup. A small taste is accentuated by delicate granules of sugar that dance on the rim and titillate my tongue.

I drink you in and become drunk with a private pleasure. My secrets are exposed like the leaves unfurled at a new dawn. As I lay in my sanctuary, perspiration glistens on my skin. I wonder how magnificent you and I might be when the fantasy touches the cool pane of reality.

While we embrace, we shall feel what has not been spoken and taste what has not been touched. Your allure in the hyacinth will be mine to explore, like the hummingbird that toils with the fluttering of its wings. Each petal shall be caressed to remember it in longing.

This well is deep, and it welcomes you to taste the freshness of its waters. Let crystalline droplets trickle between our lips and flow freely in a valley that has awaited your presence.

I am ready to receive you and the fruits that you carry. Plant seeds in my fertile soil, so that a garden of bliss blossoms for us. Let the darkness of my earth captivate you. Appreciate the richness, thereof, and stand upon the solid ground on which we shall build a home.

Toil diligently in this earth so that a righteous harvest is placed on the altar. Give me the joy and the sorrow of your days. Rest them upon my bosom. Let a sweet wine be placed by our bedside to share. Embrace me while whispers sway beneath the moon.

Slumber peacefully in my arms. For when we wake, our words are everything that we think and do. You are the sweetness of a caramel-coated candy apple that I yearn to taste when we greet one another in the secret places of seductive intelligence.

100% Organic

The physical state of our relationship is invigorating, passionate, uninhibited.
The spiritual state of our connection is enriching, affirming, intimate.
The cerebral state of our kinship is wanted, needed, relished.
The conversations are stimulating. The chemistry is great.
I like you, and it's 100% organic.

Rediscover

In a passionate moment, you said we feel amazingly familiar: the matched energy, the comfort, the natural fit of our bodies, like I was your wife in a past life.

If I failed to utter the words between my thoughts and your strokes, I agree.

Your soul's pattern is deeply pressed into my bones: the vibration reverberates through my levels of consciousness.

Certainly, I have always been – and will always be – your wife.

We meet, again, stronger and wiser this time, embracing one another with sharper senses. Give me your knowledge and allow my power to manifest our desires.

This is our time of elevation; our union is infinite.

I want you to experience everything with me: new and old, sensual and mental, carnal and astral.

Let us rediscover what we already know – together.

One Night Stand

I had a one-night stand that occurred during the day
It lasted more than two years
Prolonged booty-calls should come with extended warranties

Coronation

You are the king of the Land of Dick-Matonia
And I was dick-matized today
Please ensure that my crown and sword are bestowed
At the coronation ceremony

A Player's Fumble

You're gonna miss this
The size of my thighs
The sway of my hips

You're gonna miss those nights
Of holding on tight
To an ass that's fat, and breast just right…

To fit in your mouth

You're gonna miss the way
You would hear me say
Ooooh baby… go deeper… and deeper… and, kee… kee… keep…

Uuuumm, yeah, keep it right there

You're gonna miss when we would talk and giggle
About things that make the perfect one
And touch and caress for hours, until the other would cum…

Hard – and long – like your scepter in my temple

You're gonna miss the option of a less-conceding notion
The woman acquiesced to a more submissive motion
Like orders fulfilled by a military trooper…

Even if you were - a pooper pilot-eer

Some out there may jeer
Cuz they can't fathom the i-dear
What a stick-in-the-ass; no pun intended…

But, like I was saying, something almost ended

You're gonna miss the freak
Who sucked your dick
And loved every drop of that thick mango juice…

That I would taste on my lips; lick from my fingertips; and think
to myself about Campbells Soup: "Mmm, mmm, good"

You're gonna miss the times
We turned it out
After too much wine, too much smoking

And, oh yeah, some unmentionable places that probably shouldn't
be talked about

You're gonna miss my love
And so much more
It's 5 a.m., and I'm out the door…

Contrary to your subjective view, I have obligations to manage: a
family, conduct work, ace classes, and mourn loved ones too

You're on the chase
Of paper and tail
Making moves for you, and your homies' avail…

Our lives are full of so many things; so, I'm sure you understand,
too, why my phone might ring - at 3 a.m.

You're gonna miss this dip
That settles low
In the curve of my back…

Heaven's grace to free you of this world's mires and traps

If this was just a booty call
Then, neither one of us would trip
But you know, like I know…

That the fullness of all your blessings were missed

An opportunity for something real
Because you were too busy to slow and to see
A lover's soul; a friend's life; a true woman's individuality

You're gonna miss what you had
When your belly starts to rumble
For a plate of food; for a kiss of life; for an embrace before you
slumber…

Yeah, I think the ref said it right
He called a player's fumble

Disappointment

Gust of Arctic winds crash over me
Shears of ice slash my skin
My heart stopped beating
I let the cold sink in
What else could I do, when everything was not enough?

Upon Learning Of My Love's Betrothal

You burn in me like the towering embers at the Roman Colosseum. Brilliant flames torched high above heads, so that all may see far beyond the miles that most cannot fathom. The light intrigues many men, but none dare to rise against it.

They come to this carnal Temple in hopes to partake, jeer, or satisfy the lasciviousness that stirs deep in them... only to find themselves worthy to sit along the sidelines to raise wood or stone bits against the adversary of all it is that they desire and cannot obtain.

The heat is raw from the bleaching sun, yet I stand in your arena. Once, like a gladiator, prepared for fierce battle and carnage, willing to avenge or willing to accept blood drawn by any opponent's sword. For you, always proud; and for you, always objective to defeat.

Hence, the energy of the arena has stolen my vigor and the hardblown sands have weathered my arrogance. Now, I stand alone, as a spectacle, on the ground that the gods once whispered to be my birthplace and my birthright.

The audience appeals to me to move: to defend what is mine or to retreat in silence. But I am fixed. My strength is no longer virtuous, for my spirit is broken.

Sensing the dry cracked earth beneath my feet, I stand, awaiting the commencement words to part from your lips. None are heard, but the iron gates are raised. The scent of rich flowers and musk fill the air. My body is torn by the beast and my heart sinks, yet the embers continue to blaze in the Coliseum torches.

My soul departs long before I ever hear you speak your enchanting words of love, for they were never mine and my glory has been found in the dust.

⬥

Tangerine Moon

Standing on the edge of a bittersweet kiss, I cling to you as a tide of emotions ebb under a tangerine moon.
My feet slip on uncertain ground, and I fall into the awesomeness of everything that you are.

Warm apologies and love delicately mingle between our lips, while longing and security fill the spaces that exists between our miles and our years.
You are my rock, my world, my peace. This understanding has been acknowledged and consciously ignored for fear of loving against the odds.

We have built, together, and we have destroyed recklessly.
Nevertheless, we stand, side-by-side and face-to-face, with magnificent love that consumes all senses and binds infinitely.
I no longer fear the power that we share, so I shall continue to stand on the edge of a bittersweet kiss - knowing that you are mine - and the tangerine moon witnessed who we are.

House Music On A Sunny Day In The City

You make me remember chilled, cheap drinks on a college campus
high
Contests of power and prowess
Determining who was the best
At kickin' game; movin' fast
Making promises for calls, unkept
Nothing grounded to last

Making love outta fun
Too drunk to remember
Loud music; lookin' good; long, smoked-out nights
Oh my goodness, I think I have a contender!

House music was the pulse
Simple, unadulterated laughter with friends
Sunshine, in the midst of clouds
A joy that never ends
Those things I hold dear, like a sunny day in the city
Amongst the hustle and the bustle
And the filth in the streets
It still manages to stay pretty

Dang… Maybe this thing is a little deeper than I expected.

It's a life that existed before all things began
Our world balanced on an axis
Touched by The Creator's hand

A consummate union of polar energies, cyclical but never stopping

See the yin and the yang; the birth and the death
Understand woman and man
Loving and despising, until the world is at rest

Brother, lover, friend
Express who you are, wholly, and with no regret or shame
Knowing one's self is to understand one's world
It is all that a man has to gain

Our universe is complex, with simplicity at the core
Let me wear my nakedness gloriously before you
So that you may bask in the contradictions that much more

Refined for the masses, yet strikingly wild for your pleasure
Carpe Diem - Semper Fi
Let us live it together

I seek you out, because you inspire me
As you draw me in, I remember
House music on a sunny day
In the city
From September to September

Personal Power Questions: Lingerie

1. Is lingerie a clothing item for special occasions or everyday wear?
2. What kind of lingerie do you like and why?
3. How does lingerie make you feel when you wear it?
4. Do you wear lingerie for yourself, for your partner's liking, or both?
5. Would you feel comfortable wearing lingerie for a photo shoot? Why or why not?

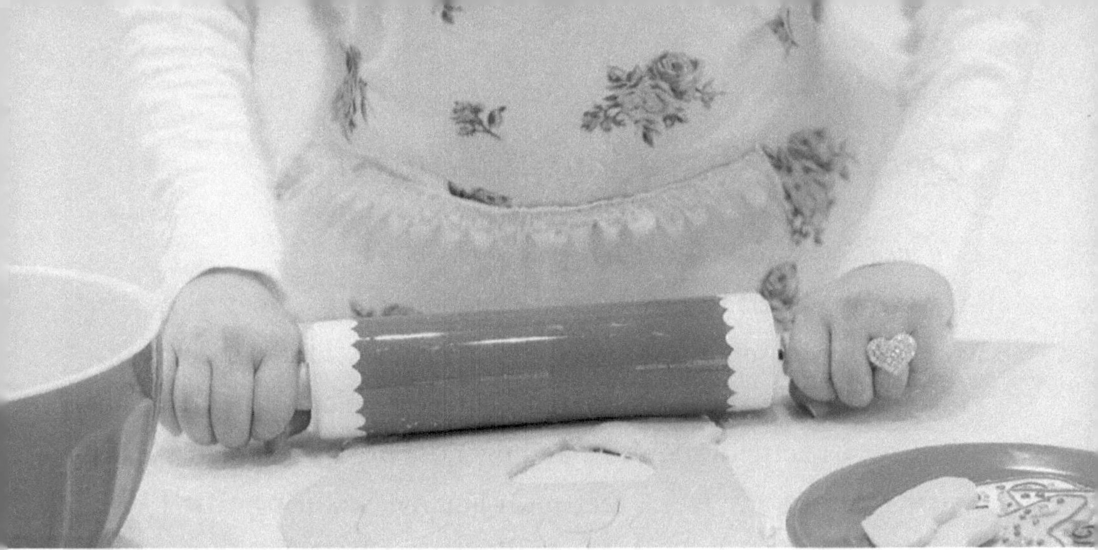

Kitchen Apron

The kitchen is a place where families and friends gather. It's the place where meals are crafted. It's the place where meaningful discussions are had. Life events like relationships, school evaluations, health concerns, family finances, planning social engagements, and so much more occur in this space. The kitchen is where trusted hands and hearts commune.

Share a meal or a moment, and feast on savory morsels. Remember to place an apron over your clothes. You might be called to help prepare a dish – or offer a valued opinion!

Childbirth: Travailing & Triumphant

~ a meditation shared with a friend 4/17/08

Carrying a child is a wonderful experience… you marvel at the changes in your body (expansion, stretch marks, limited movement, inability to see your feet, changes in skin coloration and facial features… I actually glowed… and my nose began to spread a little further across my face… feet too). For me, knowing that I was trusted to carry a child in my womb was thrilling. Feeling a child move, which often feels like gas at the onset, is thrilling. As the baby grows, it can become more uncomfortable - very similar to sleeping in bed with a small child - elbows and feet wedged into your back or stomach.

The actual signaling of the onset of childbirth was a piercing sharp pain in my abdomen. It radiated from the pit of my stomach to the middle of my back. The same sharp, piercing pains became more frequent and intense as the labor persisted: deep, severe, crushing spasms that caused me to gasp for air each time a wave of pain generated from my core and flowed over my body. Knowing that I would feel that same pain time-and-time again until my son's birth was a quiet angst. It could hardly be fathomed because my mind had no time to comprehend time and space when physical pain nearly obliterated any sense of true consciousness. And this phase was merely preparation.

The physical labor of pushing felt like my mind was physically crashing against the pain that forced itself up from my center. Debilitating pain - sucking my breath as I gasped for thin wisps of air; debilitating pain - clenching my muscles as my mind ceased to communicate with my body... the autonomic process for fight and flight was in full swing; a debilitating pain - reeling emotions that mixed between fear, anticipation, exhaustion, and joy.

It was work. It was a hard, laborious work; yet, it was a good. It was God's blessing - His ability to create such an intricate incubation process, to administer such a forlorn pain to usher new life into the world, to grant women such a strength to endure, and to give women such a special portion of grace to willfully subject themselves to such torment on many instances to see a new birth of something beautiful into this place.

After my son completed his travel through the birthing canal, a deep, warm feeling of love poured over me. Every hurt, care, or worry was gone. I knew that all was well and peace was restored. It is an awesome "labor of love."

Womanly

Friend, when you look at me and smile in a pleasing way, I respond with suspicion or a coquettish turn... yet, I feel womanly

Your words provoke thought: ideas of love, family, duty, self, spirit, and who we are. You give life to my world of rumination... and, yes, I feel womanly

When you endure my misgivings; accept my independence; encourage my progress; and provide sight where I am blind... I still feel womanly

Your reverence of my journey is appreciated: witnessing the duress of my life; buffering the wilderness that has been my home; honoring the bloom of a flower in season... and reminding me that it is okay to feel womanly

When you prepare a meal, share a glass of wine or a conversation at the close of a day... I feel womanly

Friend, your fixed presence is secure. The whispered endearments cause me to wonder about potentials that exist; about what is real and what is shit; and about what love really is. Truth lies somewhere between what is said and what is done... and I continue to feel womanly.

When I understood your position, as a man, I loved being a woman that much more.

Sister Friend

You like it cold
I like it hot
You prefer it spicy
I prefer it not

Sister-friend, you look out for me whenever you can. You lend a heart, and you also lend a hand.

My style is a bit conservative
Your style is a bit earthy
My focus is celebrating goals met
Your focus is celebrating birthdays

Sister-friend, we are different in a multitude of ways. Yet, we both cherish quality time and the tranquility of days.

You like conversations loose and rambling
I like conversations purposeful and tight
You prefer life a little bit more to the left
I prefer life a little bit more to the right

Sister-friend, I love you, and I try to express it the best way that I may. I lend an ear; I wash your clothes; and I am honored to sit with you and pray.

You like it cold
I like it hot
You prefer it spicy
I prefer it not

You are a friend, who serves double duty as a sister too. You walk; you share; and you stand with me through all the glories and all the goo.

Daddy's Burial

It was a day when the sun shined bright
The gravel groaned under the weight of the hearse
The casket rolled into the clay
And the memory of you lived in my heart

Loving my son with every fiber of my being is part of who I am. I celebrate who he is – and who he is becoming – every day.

So, You Say You're 11

Today, we celebrate your birth that happened eleven years ago. You've grown taller; you've learned a lot; and, you don't walk quite as slow.

Over these past 11 years, I've watched you do, oh, so many things, like learn to ride a bike; ask to drive up and down the pike; and, develop a love for Jordan sneakers, cologne, and rings.

My Sugar Pie, you are a wonderful boy, who is turning into a young man. Remember to stay humble, work hard, and always lend a hand.

People are judged by what they do; what they say; and, what others see. So, always strive to be a model of perfection, because it reflects on you - and it also reflects on me.

You are my biggest treasure, my greatest hope, and I love you with all my heart. I'll encourage you while you earn your success, because I've always known that you could do it from the start.

You're gonna be 11 now, and you are able to do so much more. It was fun being 10. Now, you're moving onward, through a bigger and better door!

HAPPY BIRTHDAY

Life Flashes

Mud pies, plaid coats, and hot combs
Friends in the kitchen, and Kungfu Saturdays
Blue, tan, and forest green telephones with rotary dials and twisted receiver cords
Kisses from an auntie
Broad hips and pretty dresses wrapped in aprons
Colorful ribbons and blue hair grease for the pressing comb

Wearing mom's shoes
Playing games on the porch
Running free in the grass and the streets
Red tricycles, big wheels, and wagons
Matson Run corner store and penny candy
Creek walking, fishing on a log, and sitting in the sun
Molding clay and sprinkling water
Heating kilns and swimming in the noon day

Family photographs
Daddy's camera
Newspaper-cover faces sleep on the sofa or the lounge chair
Day's events etched in black and white
Watching TV on a vibrant red carpet
Sitting in a green leather recliner
Eating pies, tasting cakes, and 7-Up soda fizz
False teeth discovered in a porcelain dish
Wigs propped in the closet recess of a bright pink room
Noonday naps
Music and melodies
Bedtime stories
Now I lay me down to sleep prayers
Black patent leather shoes

Schools, churches, parks
Bass drums and guitars
Uncle Willie's gospel group, "The Mighty Clouds of Joy"
Late-night revivals and masonic hall fundraisers for scholarships
Autumn leaves

Crisp mornings
Basketball and board games
Wisdom gained
Knowledge shared

Loving meals
Strong views and boisterous voices
Crabs by the bushels
God's presence and warm afternoons with family

Having a child is a wonderful opportunity to see the awe of creation; to peer into a future of possibilities; to behold the profound treasures of the heart; to be broken and exposed; and to always want the best of everything for another.

Son Of Mine

You were given the name meaning "gift from God." Your attribute chosen as the representation of all that you are to me, and all that you shall be to others.

A strong black man in the sallow of a transparent culture
A dignified man in the face of all that is unjust

An intelligent man, learned of the formal and the informal -
taught by text, as well as experience
A man, simply, a man

I shall love you always: extolling all that is good, real, and honorable
of your essence.
I am forever your passage, your gate - a birthright bestowed and
blessed - your mother.

I adore you

My Passage

You taught me how to learn on my own. The lessons were
undesirable, yet the education was invaluable.

Experiences were hard. Love has proved itself temperamental.
No matter. I am proven stronger than any weapon formed
against me.
Sometimes I have done the worst damage to myself.

Thank you for giving me less than what was needed.
That need was my desire to be something more.

A Mother Of Many

~Sharing a text sent to a great pastor and acquaintance, a beloved woman who is a strong mentor of women. May 2019

"A woman who you honored mentioned how you have the gift to draw out the gifts of others.

"I thought of a drawing salve – one that typically draws out infirmity.
You, however, draw the essence of each woman's divine creation stored deep in the marrow of her bones."

Green Grass & Glory

~ A memoir written at junior league football practice

Go! Go! Go! The coach blazes like a 5-alarm fire unleashed.
Oh my God! Was that my child sacked?! The mother prays, like she's confessing to a priest.

Green Grass and Glory fuels this thing. Young boy's hormones raging, while dreaming of Heisman trophies and rings.

Drop and give me 20! Don't let your knees touch the ground! Did you hear what I said son? There's no need to frown.

We're in this thing together... for better or for worse. But I've been training y'all too daggone long for you to be anything less than first!

Now understand what I'm sayin' son, 'cause this is important too. Your pride is not my concern - it is what you will – and will not do.

We're a team, and nothing less. The greatest are exalted. Work hard at what you do, and never let your spirit be halted.

When you run, I want to see the wind! And when you tackle, I want to see it rain... not the tears falling from heaven, but those of your foe, because he ought to be in pain.

Did I just hear what I heard? Did I fall and bump my head? I've been training this boy to be a gentleman, and the coach just obliterated everything I've said!

Green Grass and Glory fuels this thing. The dual nature of man is what makes him king. Ruling the Earth and dominating the field - driven by a passionate love, unbridled and unwilling to yield.

Run that ball up the field! Gain as many yards as you can! The whole time you're truckin', you better be singing, "you can't catch me... I'm the gingerbread man."

We don't have room for mistakes, or misters with lead in their britches. Take your hits like a man, 'cause you ain't gettin' no kisses... Not from me, and not from your mama. You gotta stand on your own two feet! We know it gets unsteady sometimes. That's why you wear those cleats!

We're here to play a game, son: one that requires strategy and skill. If you were a weapon of choice, I need you to be precise enough to kill!

This sport is for the brave. Even the gentleman is a brute at heart. We lust for the madness, the fury, and the mayhem that was in this from the start.

Green Grass and Glory fuels this thing. Soldiers' hopes to return valiantly from war is what the women sing.

Hold your head up son, whether we win or whether we lose. The perfection is in the battle. Being honorable is what we choose.

These boys are getting older. They must learn how to be men. Perhaps football is a rite of passage - one that kindred spirits identify deep within.

That play was magnificent! Each of you worked as part of one machine. The game plan was executed perfectly. Now, we're living the dream.

I'm not going to say it doesn't matter if we win or if we fail. I will stress - above all else - the importance of putting wind in your own sail. Your life is your boat. This team is your lesson. Give and take what's rightfully yours. All of it is a blessin'.

The long nights of practice, the broken bones, and the faces in the crowd...

When you kick that field goal or intercept a pass, raise your fist up high, and say, "look at me now!"

Some say it's savage for the namesake of a game.
I say it's Green Grass and Glory.
They were built that way all the same.

Family Ties

Family are the people who care about you; the people who support your endeavors; the people who actively participate in your life's events; the people who have your best interest at heart.

Family and relatives are not necessarily one and the same.
Knowledge is the beginning of power.
Know the difference and align yourself with those who align with you.

A Meditation On Parenting

~ Not certain to whom or why, May 6, 2005

Being a parent is tough, yet the task is rewarding in a host of ways. Parenting challenges you to be a better person by recognizing your shortcomings and doing your best not to allow them to become a part of your child's world. It invigorates you by understanding and witnessing a rare and delicate life, entrusted in your care and developed with your cultivation and nurturing. Children are lovely in every way. Being an adult can be questionable. In either respect, the role of parent will stretch you, sometimes like a medieval torture vice. It is not a task for the weak and uncommitted.

"When all the dust settles and all the crowds are gone, the things that matter are faith, family, and friends" ~Barbara Bush

Personal Power Questions: Kitchen Apron

1. With whom do you have the fondest memories of time spent in the kitchen?
2. What topics are discussed at your kitchen table?
3. When do you normally have guests in the kitchen (ex. weekly, holidays, etc.)?
4. How does your kitchen reflect an aspect of your personality?
5. Is the kitchen a place of power or influence? Why or why not?

Active Wear

When it's time to go to the gym, walk the dog, or take children to a game, what do most people wear? Active wear is an easy answer. It's the combination of running shoes, track pants, hoodies, ear buds, etc. that allow us to move with ease. The purpose of active wear is to provide ergonomic design to clothing worn for sports, exercise, and other physical activities. Women's active wear tends to be quite fashionable in addition to the function.

Purposeful action is usually engaged to make a body stronger, more flexible, and well-toned. Muscles create motion. Bones provide support. Blood circulates oxygen and other nutrients. Nerves send message to and from the brain. And the brain, itself, orchestrates everything, whether consciously or unconsciously. Sometimes we behave the same way once routine behaviors are conducted regularly. The actions are performed with very little regard, because they have become second nature. They are habitual.

In preparation of some purposeful action, let's warm-up our brains with some mental stretching. Open your mind and get ready for a workout!

A Meditation On Love

My primary education (K-12) was provided via parochial schools. As such, Catholic doctrine and the related faith practices were part of the weekly studies. These activities helped establish my foundation in Christian beliefs. They also helped create a context about how to conduct one's self at home and in the world.

One of the most popular scriptures in the Holy Bible is 1 Corinthians 13:4-8. The passage defines love and its attributes. Everything about the text indicates that love is action. The passage is quoted below. My expounded thoughts follow. Consider them and how we can love better every day.

> 1 Corinthians 13:4-8 New International Version (NIV)
>
> "**4** Love is patient, love is kind. It does not envy, it does not boast, it is not proud. **5** It does not dishonor others, it is not self-seeking, it is not easily angered, it keeps no record of wrongs. **6** Love does not delight in evil but rejoices with the truth. **7** It

always protects, always trusts, always hopes, always perseveres.

8 Love never fails. But where there are prophecies, they will cease; where there are tongues, they will be stilled; where there is knowledge, it will pass away."

LOVE IS...
*Patient. Therefore, it waits
*Kind. Therefore, it is compassionate, gentle
*Not Envious. Therefore, it celebrates other's success
*Not Boastful. Therefore, it is quiet... not loud
*Not Proud. Therefore, it is humble... not seeking approval for acts
*Not Dishonoring. Therefore, it is obedient and polite... respectful
*Not Self-Seeking. Therefore, it shares the best with others
*Not Easily Angered. Therefore, it is balanced, even, well-tempered
*Not a Keeper of Wrongs. Therefore, it gives praise
*Not Delighted in Evil, but rejoices in the peace and righteousness of the truth

LOVE ALWAYS...
*Protects. Therefore, it provides care and secure holding for things of value
*Trusts. Therefore, it knows all is well - or that a situation will turn out well
*Hopes. Therefore, it imagines the best in all people and circumstances
*Perseveres. Therefore, it works diligently and continually toward success

LOVE AMENDS & ASCENDS

Legacy

Each of us is gifted with something unique. One of my gifts is the ability to express deep thought and emotion through writing. What I write is a work to honor God. Sharing truth in the distinct voice that was given to me is my honor. May the sound reverberate through time, open and/or resonate with someone else's path, and exist as part of a meaningful legacy.

As all things are connected, where shall we intersect?

Conscious

Thought is energy, the beginning of formation. Word is life, the process of manifestation. Emotion is vibration, the movement of neurochemical station.

Collective consciousness is co-creation, a concept only grasped when you speak the native tongue of the people. We shall pray, meditate, share energy, or perhaps focus thought. Fashioned in circles or lined in pews, we are one: God-like. If made in the image of an infinite and divine being, we also are infinite and divine. As it was in the beginning, now, and ever shall be, world without end, amen, amen.

We are the spirits embodied in water, in fire, in earth, and in wind. We are the stars of the zodiac; the logic of the numbers; the intuition of the cards; the patterns of the sacred geometry; the children of God. We are spirit, created and re-created in this life – this dimension – this plane – as well as the place in – and beyond – the heaven, the hell, the purgatory, and the darkness.

Thought knew us before we knew ourselves. We elevate from one spiritual plane to the next, until we remember what we forgot.

Tranquility

It is the hum of kitchen appliances late at night
The warmth found in the crevice of a lover's arm
Peace in knowing your Creator's power
Warm sun shining while sitting on a park bench

It is a heaven found in miles that distance distress
Children's laughter
Quiet meditation to calm the soul
A drawn bath scented with lavender and rose oils

It is sips of champagne by candlelight
Jazz music floating on a hot summer breeze
Sleeping on crisp cotton sheets
Baby's breath on your shoulder

It is sharing a meaningful conversation by simply saying nothing
Knowing a secret is safe with a friend
Tasting a fresh snowfall
Loving life and self without reservation

---

*Do accessories matter when wearing active wear? Pearls offer an
air of refinement. Diamonds mesmerize with sparkle and flair.
Distinguishing watches are a great conversation piece too. The
important question is if you want to subject your fine accessories to any
potential damage that may occur as you move throughout the day?*

Indomitable

As I get closer to my purpose, what feels like stumbles, back-
peddling, circumvents, and knock downs, are viewed through the
spiritual eye as agility, dancing, scenic travel, and repositioning.
Perspective builds the mental and emotional strength to start
anew.

Color Struck

Blue moved me today
It picked me up and sat me down in a serene place
The mood was mellow

Blue's hue was calm and cool
It felt like a spring breeze after a noon day shower
The moment was clean

Blue spoke to me like my daddy did when I was a little girl
It had baritones that were slow and deep
The comfort was careless, like a misplaced chord on a familiar melody

Blue's depth was remarkable
It offered tranquility
The simplicity was a delight

Time Traveler

Drums and heat beat against the hot desert plains
Rhythms of music - life - and fear - glisten on the evergreen floor of the Amazon

Richness flows through the valley of waters, both crimson and clear
Providing sustenance to those things upward-bounding: mountains, foliage, eyes, and arms

Reach for the universe.

A babe is kissed by the stars and the moon
New life is presented to the spirits in homage of the ancestry: a link to the future
Hope is poured through the fragrant oils that spill over the head and touch the mind
Something sacred has entered this place – energy added

Move to a higher level with binary and tertiary cohesion.

Dark skin transverses across the waters and the lands
Exploring the richness of everything that is God-given
Blissful gardens exist of which to dwell... to meditate... to cultivate… to grow…
Seeds of knowledge and wisdom sprout forth

Understand self by recognizing the Divine within.

A deep concentration of melanin is diluted by the travels across space and time
Terrain becomes cold and hard; the water flows slowly
Air is thinned by the altitude; oxidized life becomes parasitic
Attempts to move closer to little gods exiles us from our true nature: we become weak

Listen to lies too long and they become truth.

Eternity is in the soul, yet clocks constrict an infinite state
Vastness is minimized... to years, months, days, hours, minutes,
and seconds
Time - moving in a linear fissure, swirling in a constant vortex –
folding in on itself - continually

Reconstitution degrades the effectiveness of what was originally
done.

Clothes. Hair Styles. Women. Men.
Wars. Discussions. Reparations. Peace.
Nothing has changed, yet everything looks different

Time travels on...

Pan-African

Melanin moves in concentric circles to find a path forged by faith.
Mother, father, great, and grand – lineages embrace darkness to
engage in a fearful fantasy.
Stolen children, whispers, wisdom, and songs speak of a freedom
lost.
Power and essence corrupted by a savage hunger of the recessive
child.

Deprivation of community and security, those things woven through family ties, proper education, good health, and opportunity, prepare us not for success, but instead systematic destruction.

What lies before us is undetermined; what lies behind us is nearly forgotten.

Eloquent native, remember your path of greatness birthed from the Nile to now.

The pale light of ignorance flickers - and it shall be consumed by darkness.

⸻◦◦◦⸻

Active engagement requires physical conditioning (for movement) and critical thinking (for strategy). Routine fasting is needed to balance the metabolism and the spirit. Sleep allows the body to restore itself after exertion… Slumber also keeps people unaware of important activity. Be aware of media hype. The message may be a distraction.

⸻◦◦◦⸻

Insomnia

Books, food, telephone calls, and television no longer suffice.

Why is it like this?

Blares from an electronic trumpet greet the sun.

My senses are touched with charismatic chatter of morning hosts and popular music that fill the uncongested corners of my room.

A new day dawns with freshness slowly slipping down tall blades
of grass.
Sleeplessness surrendered to a misty twilight.
The breaking day left fragments of a surreal, stained-glass dream
on my windowpane.
Rise with the heads of the tulips and declare a glorious morning
with a cup of joe.

❦

*Random thoughts ramble. String them along, and
you can make meaningful connections. Is that a
function of Divine Spirit or self-imposed will?*

❦

The Apocalypse Of The Capitalist Slumber Party

When pin-striped pigs and lollipops fly, it's in my dreams
The hills are alive with the sound of music
Another figment of my mind
Grocery lists, doodles, to-do memos
Eyes roll to the back of heads
Others simply drop
Pontification flowing as blue and black pens tap

Hmmm, I like those shoes. Are they Kenneth Cole's or Jimmy Choo's?

Another alluring distraction
Spider in the corner
Dust drifting from fluorescent lights
Foot taps and shifting bodies buffered by carpeted floors and upholstered seats
Group participation needed for think tanks and coverups
The long hours of the nights don their keep

Another corporate meeting, useless at its apex.

People and ideas seeking to look like more
Red tape identifies precautions
A bureaucratic wasteland of ash exists
Pay credit or swipe debit, both transparent transgressions to the FICO score
Accountability is dismissed with dollars
Zombies walk from the Hoodoo Bayou
They stand heartless at America's doors, waiting to devour truth
And bleed lies that kill like airborne contagion

There are days, even seasons in life, that seem overwhelming.
God knows a financial crunch can bring a ton of stress.
Life happens! Monthly bills, activities for children, family

vacations, date night... And then, an unexpected crisis occurs. Then, another one rolls right around the corner.

Mastering money management can help reduce stress. It also offers power and influence at various levels – in your personal affairs, as well as mobility within your community. How powerful are you? How powerful would you like to be? Master self. Master giving. Paradise can be part of every day. Blood, sweat, and tears are only one side of the coin. Refreshing water, a natural glow, and joy are on the other side of that same coin. Flip it!

Bleeding

There are days when it feels like all you do is bleed money

I'm glad I have enough today to let it flow... No adhesives or sutures needed

I might even be able to offer an intravenous line for someone else

It is known that bleeding too much can cause hemorrhaging

Hemophilia is not desired

Donate a few ounces to sustain another's life

Save a few pints of blood to maintain your own

Vampires will let blood until the arteries and veins are dry

Relationships happen at all levels: personal, professional, communal, and global. Ideally, a relationship should add value to each member participating. To that end, it is worthy to evaluate the relationships in your life regularly. Ensure that benefits and values exist in your relationships. Benefits are the incentives (or positive results) of the relationship, like increased revenue, emotional support, a monthly newsletter. Values, on the other hand, are the core principles that guide your lifestyle, like family first, no harm to animals or the environment, and religious preferences.

When a relationship assessment identifies a lack of fulfillment, it is time to change the nature of the relationship. Negotiate new terms that work for everyone involved or end the interaction. Offering a KISS (Keep It Simple and Straightforward) makes it easy. Many know that I am a kisser, by nature, literally and figuratively!

A Shared Thought With My Love

"I strive for deliberation in my thoughts and actions. For me, emotions are an internal regulator/reflection of core thoughts, expectations, and the integrity and balance thereof. My engagement with you has been deliberate. There is meaning; there is purpose; and I value it. This is a time for me to heal and elevate – and you nurture that in many ways. I want it to continue. Ideally, I offer the same to you."

Being a cerebral person in a society that rarely nurtures thought can feel restrictive. The following excerpt was part of an email dialogue sent to a great co-worker in 2001.

Simply Thinking

"I've learned that practicality and rationality can become a means of avoiding passion. The detachment allows an individual to be objective about a relationship but, that individual is no longer involved in the relationship.

I speak from my own experience; and I realize that the things that I value: my "individuality," my "separateness," my "autonomy," and my "liberated woman-ness" have overruled the essence of my growth. I cannot grow unless I interact... interact with the people places and things that I ultimately love, like, and despise. To one degree or another, all these things create the passionate beings that we are.

My spirit has been bruised when I've approached matters in a passionate way. I speak of passion in the way of emotion-felt, purposeful, action. My pain was evoked when the same passion was not returned to me.

I had a recent revelation when I spoke to an acquaintance of mine. He read the same poem that I allowed you to read, and he advised me to exude my faith, strength, and love and all things so that I exemplify what God had intended.

By far, I am not a religious person; however, I am a very spiritual one. By saying so, I lead into this following principal: energy that is expelled is returned and/or recreated in some shape or form. I would love to discuss philosophy to any degree, but now is not the time.

In following, the things that you give freely are the things that you receive freely. The passionate parts of yourself - that you cleave to yourself - cannot be enjoyed because they are preserved so securely.

My amnesia has diluted my consciousness and my spirit for many years, but I'm beginning to remember me. I would hope that you don't deny yourself in the manner that I have because it affords much more grief and angst than one person should bear."

I attended a writing workshop in Roswell, Georgia on February 8, 2007. The facilitator gave a creative writing exercise. Each attendee was tasked with describing the person sitting to his or her right side. A middle-aged woman sat next to me. This was my observation, up-close and intimate.

People Watching

She reminds me of the Geechee mulatto: a glowing complexion, bronzed by the sun. The warmth of her honey-colored eyes express warmth and happiness. An underlying melancholy rest behind the sweetness of her smile.

Initial eye contact is uncomfortable: perhaps afraid it might reveal too much - or not enough. The windows to her soul are guarded by a frequent opening and shutting of the blinds. Eventually, the post guard's arms get weary. The sudden blinks become slower. The high, flushed cheekbones relax.

She is a woman on guard, pleasantly waiting for you at the gate, but yielding to any new entry. Caution is hers. Love emanates always.

A good line of vision is needed for any activity. If needed, correct the vision with contact lenses, surgery, or glasses. Have you ever heard the euphemism that hindsight is 20/20? It implies that foresight can be unclear at times. Looking back can reveal areas that could have been avoided or areas that need improvement for future function.

Sharing experiences for the sake of comradery, knowledge, and strength is the premise. Let the power of a woman's wardrobe inspire you! Even a nice pair of spectacles can be an interesting accessory!

7 Steps To Easier Living

❖ Avoid injury and uncomfortable situations when possible for self – and for others.

❖ Be flexible

❖ Don't gripe and gossip. Offer solutions to a problem (otherwise, hold your wagging tongue).

❖ When a wrongdoing has occurred, acknowledge it; offer a genuine apology; and fix the problem for reconciliation.

❖ Look for the lesson in all experiences. Something good can come from a bad experience.

❖ Be insightful and creative. Know when to discard or repurpose broken things (ex. items, relationships, thoughts, and habits).

❖ Streamline every area of your life for optimized efficiency, productivity, output, and return. Don't waste valuable resources (time, money, skill, people, or emotion).

Personal Power Questions: Active Wear

1. Do you participate in a daily activity to further your learning of some sort?

2. Who in you circle of influence serves as a mentor to you?

3. How often are your critically thinking about the information set before you?

4. Where can you volunteer 4-10 hours per month in your community?

5. What piece of active wear do you consider most important and why?

Church Lady Hat

What image comes to mind when you think about a spiritual woman? A big-brimmed hat trimmed in satin or chiffon is my first mental image. When attending church events and fancy fundraisers with my family, as a young girl, many of the women wore what was affectionately called the "church lady hat." It often blocked the view of the on-looker. There was nothing to be seen of the pastor at the podium; the awards being granted, the choir singing; or any other activity that should have been viewable by a spectator. Typically, all you could expect to see were curls of hair, either plaited, pinned or trailing from a big ol' hat that blocked the view!

Another image of a spiritual woman that comes to mind is a lady dressed in a long, flowing gown that billows in a breeze. Her countenance is centered and peaceful. She is calm with wisdom and experience. That woman is the one I want to know. She is neither moved nor impressed by pomp and circumstance; titles and hierarchy; or rote religious practices and dogma. She is a woman who knows her worth. She is woman, as creator, and woman, reflector of light. She is a divine image of the Most High. In my mindfulness, this woman is the one I strive to be.

Women operate in a multitude of roles. They are skilled in cottage industry, managing domestic affairs and offices, economic trade, midwifery, agriculture, spiritual life, and much more. The scope has been revered, and the scope has been reviled – in cultures and ages, both old and new. May a woman's inner guidance continue to influence and increase her outer territory. In my study, the Proverbs 31 woman is the standard.

The Proverbs 31 Woman
The Holy Bible, Proverbs 31:10-31 (New International Version)

"Epilogue: The Wife of Noble Character
10 A wife of noble character who can find?
She is worth far more than rubies.
11Her husband has full confidence in her
and lacks nothing of value.
12She brings him good, not harm,
all the days of her life.
13She selects wool and flax
and works with eager hands.
14She is like the merchant ships,

bringing her food from afar.
15She gets up while it is still night;
she provides food for her family
and portions for her female servants.
16She considers a field and buys it;
out of her earnings she plants a vineyard.
17She sets about her work vigorously;
her arms are strong for her tasks.
18She sees that her trading is profitable,
and her lamp does not go out at night.
19In her hand she holds the distaff
and grasps the spindle with her fingers.
20She opens her arms to the poor
and extends her hands to the needy.
21When it snows, she has no fear for her household;
for all of them are clothed in scarlet.
22She makes coverings for her bed;
she is clothed in fine linen and purple.
23Her husband is respected at the city gate,
where he takes his seat among the elders of the
land.
24She makes linen garments and sells them,
and supplies the merchants with sashes.
25She is clothed with strength and dignity;
she can laugh at the days to come.
26She speaks with wisdom,
and faithful instruction is on her tongue.
27She watches over the affairs of her household
and does not eat the bread of idleness.

28Her children arise and call her blessed;
her husband also, and he praises her:
29"Many women do noble things,
but you surpass them all."
30Charm is deceptive, and beauty is fleeting;
but a woman who fears the Lordis to be praised.
31Honor her for all that her hands have done,
and let her works bring her praise at the city gate."

The One Who Loves Me Best

I hear You speak to me in the quiet of the night, while the darkness comforts me like a blanket. I lay close to You, my bare skin caressing an abounding plain.

Wind chimes whisper to my unconscious. They guide me to a place where colors seduce my soul. Lapis, jade, and amethyst dreams float beyond what I can see and pass through an effervescent state.

You touch me in a way that makes my body tremble. Tears of joy spill from my eyes.

I am unable to escape all that You will for me to have.

I am open. You make love to my mind, greeting me anxiously with passion and admiration. You place me upon a pedestal. I am Your priestess, sacred as Your temple.

Our love is exalted at the alter – a communion that we share before all. Prayer binds us together. Faith dismantles menacing ties.

You love me when I turn away from You, soiling myself with the lusts of my carnal heart. I defile the sacred ground that You apportion for me, adorning myself with cheap trinkets and men.

My blood sheds, warm and thick. It marks my status of womanhood. It reminds me of Africa and its tributaries that flow. Riches are buried deep in the fertile crescent; yet, warfare rages in the spiritual and the physical realms. Struggle for principality and place exist.

You are steadfast, and You are awesome. You wash me clean and offer provisions in the wrath of my despair. Your strength and dedication are undeniable as You carry my fears, my transgressions, and my bitterness until I realize that they are of no use. Your benevolence is extraordinary. Despite my waywardness, You continually bestow lavish gifts and lovely robes to remind me of my divine beauty and godly origins.

My wants and needs are always satisfied, without reservation and in great abundance. You love me as You love Yourself, and it culls my desire to please You.

Grooming and maturity were needed. The young girl is now a woman, prepared to expand the kingdom of The One who loves her best. Lord, You are worthy.

Vessels

Give honor to our mothers and fathers, the vessels who brought us through (part of the lineage before them). It is a sacred act in honoring God. Give homage to the root of our being.

Body Mystique

Your body is a temple
An edifice to the Most High
It's intricate cuts, curves, and crevices are unique
Ones that only The Creator can defy

A temple is uniquely built
From the inside, to the out
It's magnificence is undeniable
The Master Architect's work
Simply perfect, no creature can doubt

The body is a temple
Sacred, a reserve for El Elyon's joy
Let the rites of a young girl be separate
A distinctive counterpart to the rites of a young boy

Learn to respect the temple
It is a slow and gracious practice

Let the love of God and the love of Self
Be the balance of the axis

Teeter not; surrender none
Be not guiled by the wiles of the world outside your doors
For thieves, liars, murderers and the unsavory
Find contentment with the likes of whores
Those who do not understand the temple, will share the altar
With fragrant spice
Idolaters of money, of power, of sex and of sins
Will blaspheme with their despicable cries

Evil-doers barge into the temple
Bringing rapture against God's will
As they surround and encroach upon the light within
Remain peaceful and prayerful still

A woman may mistake a man who stands boldly at the door
As the temple's awaited priest
She grants him privilege to move freely within
Yet he consumes like that of the beast

Yield not your temple to anyone
Without the holy counsel for which you were made
Take refuge in the flourishing branches of knowledge
Wisdom and prudence shall provide the needed shade

Young men yearn to boast of their temples' strength
A fortress imperious and unbending
Let not the sly tongue and the seductive ways of a woman's cunning
Cause brake and need for mending

Keep your temple clean and keep it sanctified
For it is holy, the home of spirit
Let it look good, smell good, be good
As your morning bell rings for all to hear it

Bodies are our temples
Keeping them well is an act of worship
Forever, unto the Most High
The head, the chest, the limbs, the feet – eternally until we die

---

Your 1, 2, 3, 4, 5, 6, 7, 8, And 9

Patiently, I wait for you
Expecting directive, showing me what to do
Aptly, I put away old things
Clearing ideas, clearing space, a desire of learning something new

I am patient, as patient as I think I can be
All the while, I wait, wondering what you have in store for me

Did I do it right?
Must I live it again?
Is this another lesson from a foolish act?
I close my eyes and say, "Amen"

You have loved me, and graciously, You have taught me many
things
Don't cast your pearls before swine
And women of virtue shall be adorned with rings

My earthly cloth has been stripped
And my worldly mind has been rested
As I put more faith in You, all the more is tested

Children lose their way
The country's people lose their homes
Love's strength dilutes to a trickle
And broken spirits cry and moan

Lord, help me to remember
That I am continually blessed through You
There is nothing that can not be achieved, overcome, or transformed
When it is Your will to do

"Thy kingdom come, thy will be done…"
Through me or any other vessel whom you see fit
Help me temper my tongue; strengthen my walk; and fix my mind
So that I may always be inside of it

Your kingdom is my home – it is here; it is now
Give me voice to make it known, and grant me peace as I imagine
and create the days through
As I am perfect in Your vision
I am always a reflection of You

Your child
Your spirit
Your 1, 2, 3, 4, 5, 6, 7, 8, and 9

~ The following reflection was based on an activity done at my old worship center in Alpharetta Georgia. Our Bible study group was reviewing Chapter 23 in the book of Psalms. This Psalm is one of David's songs to the Lord, expressing how God sustained him despite the reigning king's intent to pursue and kill David. This psalm is often read during funerals, as part of a death ritual; however, it has a wonderfully broad context for life as well.

Each Bible study member was tasked to read the passage and write his/her own interpretation of Psalm 23 as it reflects their personal relationship with God.

Below, you shall find the original Psalm 23, followed by my interpretation, entitled, "Who God is to Me." drafted on February 7, 2007:

Psalms 23, Bible (KJV)
A psalm of David.
The Lord is my shepherd; I shall not want.
2 He maketh me to lie down in green pastures: he leadeth me beside the still waters.
3 He restoreth my soul: he leadeth me in the paths of righteousness for his name's sake.

4 Yea, though I walk through the valley of the shadow of death, I will fear no evil: for thou art with me; thy rod and thy staff they comfort me.

5 Thou preparest a table before me in the presence of mine enemies: thou anointest my head with oil; my cup runneth over.

6 Surely goodness and mercy shall follow me all the days of my life: and I will dwell in the house of the Lord for ever.

Who God Is To Me

The Lord is my sculptor. I am a beautiful reflection of Him.

He made every rough and smooth pattern to uniquely reflect the light. My form is pliable - for His pleasure - so that I may bend and move, but never break.

Man-made crafter's tools of metal, stone, and acid pummel against my surface, but they do not damage my finish. For the Lord, God, sealed me with a heavenly coat.

You prepare a pedestal for me - setting me above my enemies. Certainly, they revel at Your work and know that Your craftsmanship cannot be matched.

As it is well, goodness and love will remain with me. I am an exhibit in your gallery. True beauty and splendor shall be revealed when I see Your face.

The Color Of Godliness

Is red the color of godliness?
Hot. Passionate. Fiery.
The shade of love: deep and womb-like.
Bloods hue: thick and viscous.
Red's rage: turbulent and spilling over boundaries and ages.
It's fullness swells in the hearts of men, flowing with compassion
and burning with Hell's fury.

Could the color of godliness be embodied in orange's fraction?
Warm. Robust. Full.
The pigment of harvests: yielding fruit from the toil of the land
and bounty for diligent work.

A cornucopia's presence: matured and transitioned to a place of
quiet contemplation.
Orange's delight: complacent and prepared for peace.
God's day of rest surely appeared upon on a horizon, delicately
balanced between crimson and wheat.

Can yellow express the color of godliness?
Innocent. Fresh. Light.
The tinge of suggestion: ribbons for those who support a desert
war and the young girl's virginity that sways above the hemline.
Sunshine's rays: abounding and ablaze.

Yellow's fondness: reminiscent and suspended in a haze of golden flecks.

Honor your ancestors in the sallow and the strength of their wills.

Might the color of godliness be green as the grass beneath our feet?
Fortune. Life. Newness.

The shade of envy: deeply rooted and covered with transparent facades.

Amazon foliage: lush and uncharted.

Green's renewed spirit: faithful and expecting nothing less than greatness.

Be ye a new creature to roam the Earth.

Why should blue not be attributed to the color of godliness?
Powerful. Deep. Heavenly.

The symbol of family: heirlooms and crests among the Northern conquests.

Velvet's texture: soft and comforting.

Blue's loftiness: resting among the stars that shine in the night.

Gem-crusted ephods for priest who employ mystical knowledge, yet sober when humanity fails it's God-like form.

Does the color of godliness exude in indigo's electric presence?
Vibrant. Imaginative. Glowing.

The hue of potential: charismatic and exponential.

A wildflower: while random in the field, it calls the eye to take notice.

Indigo's creativity: dwelling in both Divine and human form.

Humble self to acknowledge the Spirit in in the midst; pay homage with blissful offerings.

How then is violet able to represent the color of godliness?

There is no rule of structure, as it is full consciousness, activated.

A mark of kings: the combination of red's humanity and blue's Heavenly ether.

The designation of leaders; royalty defined.

It is a virtuous woman garb, setting her apart in wisdom and in works.

Keep that which is holy prepared for battle or retreat.

Allow the sanctified banner to wave in the winds of change.

A distinctive aroma fills the nostrils of those who are chosen for anointing - the blessed herbs prepared in the virgin oil of the olive.

Do not turn away from the knowledge that was given in the Garden of Eden.

Mastery supersedes destruction when abilities are exercised with proper perspective and heart: that of prosperity, equity, and excellence - not only to your fellow man but most importantly to God.

So, what shall we decree as the color of godliness?

All these things are the color of Godliness: light fragmented; sound vibrating; emotion activated; and consciousness creating pigments to which we ascribe meaning.

Personal Power Questions: Church Lady Hat

1. What is spirituality to you?
2. When did you experience your first spiritual moment (good or bad)?
3. How do spiritual practices make you feel empowered?
4. Who makes you feel most connected to others or the universe?
5. Where do you identify challenges with spirituality or spiritual practices?
6. Why is spirituality important or unimportant in your life?

Consider The Construction

Women fight for the virtue of their lives continually. It happens every day - in every environment. Bedrooms, board rooms, battle fields, birthing centers, and ballot boxes are just a few places to mention. How does each power suit look?

More importantly, do you know how the power suit was constructed? Appreciating the quality of the material offers a unique pride in the workmanship. This remark can be literal or figurative. Nonetheless, the power of a woman's wardrobe is amazing!